THE MIDDLE AGES

A History from Beginning to End

Copyright © 2016 by Hourly History.

All rights reserved.

Table of Contents

The Early Middle Ages
Advancing to Empire with Charlemagne
The High Middle Ages
The Flowering of the Church
Times of Change
The Late Middle Ages
The End and the Beginning
Conclusion
About the Author

Chapter One
The Early Middle Ages

For too long, many people, including some scholars, saw these two periods of history as the seminal epochs in civilization's history. In between? Only the Middle Ages, a long interim period also known as the Dark Ages. However, historians are rethinking the significance of this time period stretching from 476 CE, when the Roman Empire in the West was reduced by vigorous barbarians to a glorious memory, and the outbreak of intellectual inspiration that led to a rebirth of art, creativity, and even national politics around the 14th century. It's true that the Renaissance was a glittering panoply of achievement, but that doesn't mean that the Middle Ages had nothing to bring to civilization's table: what about Charlemagne, Richard the Lionheart, Eleanor of Aquitaine, Magna Carta and the Peasants' Revolt? What about Joan of Arc? The Black Death? Cathedrals with soaring architecture, illuminated manuscripts that inspired, literary legends that have endured all attest to the dynamic artistry, productivity, and significance of the era that is so much more than the centuries packed in between Rome's fall and the Renaissance's flowering.

This period of time is so shrouded in mystery that it's often difficult to discern where truth ends and myth begins. It was during this time, somewhere in the fifth century, that historians believe that a warlord in England rallied his forces to protect against the Saxon invasion. In later centuries, the story of Arthur would be embellished into the legend of Camelot and the tales would inspire the courts, troubadours, and artists of the later Middle Ages. Some credit a Briton of Roman habits named Arcturus with inspiring his people in the fifth century into a sense of nationalism; others say there was a man of Welsh background who fought against the Saxons who had been invading and encroaching on English lands. Later, the brief, shining hour of legend was temporary; the Anglo-Saxons came to dominate the island until they, in turn, were defeated by the Scandinavian Vikings and later by the Normans. A great deal of cultural recycling took place during the Middle Ages as the hardy peoples built on and bettered what was at hand.

Some of the mystery is solved by what archeologists found in the Sutton Hoo burial site which dates from the sixth and early seventh centuries. The artefacts from the ship burial include a helmet, shield and sword, a lyre, a suite of metalwork dress fittings in gold and jewels, and silver plate. The grave tells much about these peoples and how they lived, and history is indebted to archeology for filling in some of the missing pieces. However, additional missing pieces remain, nonetheless.

It's not as if there was an immediate and abrupt schism between the time when Rome fell and the nations that they'd conquered were left to fend for themselves. The society of the Middle Ages was divided in three sectors: laborers, warriors, and clerics. Farmers continued to plant seeds and pray for a good harvest even as the prayers to the one God of the Christians replaced the many gods who had ruled over the elements. A local landowner who assumed the military responsibility for protecting his estate continued to do so, albeit without the overarching protection of Rome. The Christian Church, once it had won the hearts and souls of Europeans, would grow to be the entity that would provide spiritual solace, inspire the arts, and recruit for religious wars over the course of time. But first, the orphaned nations had to deal with the pains of growing up.

The Middle Ages are generally regarded as lasting from the fifth to the fifteenth century, although the latter date is more fluid depending on the country. However, the Middle Ages represent so complex a span of time that the centuries must be divided into separate eras in order for the times to correctly and accurately be analyzed.

The Early Middle Ages began in 476 with the fall of the Roman Empire and lasted until roughly 1000 CE, give or take a century here and there.

The High Middle Ages spanned the three centuries from 1000 to 1300.

The Late Middle Ages, the period that bordered the beginning of the Renaissance, started in 1300 and ended around 1450.

The Middle Ages were rooted in their Roman past, but what blossomed from the soil of the Empire, proved to be a bold and bright flower that would reveal humanity in such depth and nuance that it unleashed the power of mortal creativity to express it, even as its survival in the early years was precarious.

The End of the Empire

In 60 BCE, Julius Caesar began a period of conquest and power consolidation that would result in the creation of the mighty Roman Empire. Roman rule, extending from the British Isles, all of the Mediterranean region, northwestern Europe, the Near East, northern Africa, and Palestine, controlled a stretch of territory that today encompasses 48 countries. Roman roads were renowned for their efficiency and for their role in encouraging trade. The disciplined soldiers of the Roman legions were unbeatable; Roman law was supreme, and the fabled Pax Romana was a peace enforced by the knowledge of what Roman might was capable of doing. The Empire was an ethnic melting pot made up of every demographic from sophisticated Greeks to provincial Celts. In the West, Latin was the formal language; in the East, Greek. This would prove significant in the centuries to come in the West, when Latin retained its mastery.

Before the Empire's demise, the dangers from that earlier Wild West were already becoming apparent. The Emperor Diocletian divided the Empire into two segments, the Eastern and Western Empires; Emperor Constantine took matters a dramatic step further when he made Constantinople in the East the capital of the Empire instead of Rome. Roman citizenship was no longer the hard-to-achieve symbol of belonging; full citizenship was granted to all the Empire's subjects who were free. Although Rome imposed its laws upon subject nations, those nations were not expected to emulate Roman dress, food, or customs, so they retained their own identities. Those identities would become distinct after the Empire fell, and nations which had considered themselves part of Rome realized that they were on their own.

Despite the dominance of the Empire, there were enemies beyond the borders. Germanic tribes joined forces to attack the Empire and acquire territory. In 410, Alaric, king of the Visigoths, led a sack of Rome; in 455, it was the Vandals threatening the city. The Western Empire was vulnerable on its western borders. Huns, Goths, Visigoths, Picts, and Scots repeatedly hammered the boundaries. In order to protect its borders, Rome allowed some of its Germanic foes to settle Roman lands in exchange for maintaining the borders against other barbarian enemies. Vandals ruled Spain and the remaining Roman provinces in northern Africa; Ostrogoths were in Dalmatia, and Huns held power in Eastern Europe. The invaders took the axiom "When in Rome, do like the Romans" seriously. The Empire was glue for disparate tribes and peoples, even as they retained their own customs and languages. Everyone wanted to be Roman, and even the barbarians—which meant anyone who wasn't Roman—who were hired to fight for Roman became Romans: the Visigoths in Spain, the Vandals in North Africa, the Ostrogoth in Italy; the Franks in France, the Angles, Saxons and Danes who settled in England. And they fought against the Huns who attacked Rome in 451.

The Emperor Justinian did his best, recapturing North Africa from the Vandals, Italy from the Ostrogoths and some of Spain from the Visigoths, but these were tough battles, made even more debilitating when the bubonic plague, broke out in Constantinople, spreading across

Europe and leaving death in its path. The plague would make another, even more lethal appearance centuries later, but the toll it took on the Empire was a burden impossible to bear.

Finally, the Empire was too weak to last. Odoacer revolted against Roman rule, deposing the emperor. In 476, the last Roman emperor, Romulus Augustulus died, leaving the Germanic Odoacer to be declared king of Italy. Rome had fallen. Its successors had the example of Rome but not its order.

But what did survive, and what would become the bastion of learning, power and administrative order in the West was the Christian Church. Once the despised sect persecuted by the authorities, the Christian Church had risen to power under Constantine. After the cohesiveness of the Empire eroded, there was nothing that could provide stability - except the Church. Christendom, or Europe after the fall of Rome, was regarded as a blend of the ecclesiastical hierarchy and the political leaders. Pope and emperor balanced the sacred and the secular.

The Empire and its protection were gone - but religion remained.

The Monasteries and the Early Middle Ages

As the Empire declined, the power vacuum required something to take its place. That something was Christianity. The old gods were not completely gone, but the Christian faith, invigorated, dynamic, and proselytizing since its inception over four hundred years earlier, was ready to supplant them with a unifying doctrine of miracles, mysticism, and fervent belief. As the faith had spread, it had inspired many different means of practice. From the earliest years, monasticism, where believers went to live in either solitude or community with other Christians dedicated to a life of spirituality and service, had been representative of Christianity throughout the fourth, fifth, and sixth centuries.

As monasteries grew, their role become more integrated into the communities where they were established. The lords of the manor had use for the monasteries. They sent their children to be educated there; those second sons who would not inherit the title were encouraged to become clerics. In return, their wealthy parents endowed the monasteries. The church profited financially from its spiritual rule, as it was exempt from taxation and people were expected to tithe ten percent of their income.

But monasteries did not only affect the spiritual aspect of life. The monks were skilled in the use of herbs, caring for the ill and providing medical care. They had agricultural knowledge, and their talents aided the development of, among other things, Benedictine liquor, Trappist beer, and Dom Perignon. Monasteries promoted education and learning, teaching their young scholars arithmetic, religion, and grammar. What they could not teach, of course, was how to protect the community. That decidedly secular job fell to men who had the means and skills to bear arms.

Religion was discovering its power base. As the orphaned nations of West struggled to survive, with only the Christian Church offering a unifying link, another religion was also forming a cohesive order in the Arabian

Peninsula, where Muhammed's introduction of Islam was spreading swiftly. Muhammed died in 632 but the armies of Allah conquered the Middle East, uniting the population under a caliph and providing spiritual comfort for a faith that at the height of its range ruled over a world three times larger than the entirety of Christendom. The impassioned faithful of the two creeds were destined to meet on hostile terms.

Chapter Two

Advancing to Empire with Charlemagne

The political turmoil of the era made life precarious for ordinary citizens who had enough to deal with simply trying to eke out a living from the land. Regardless of who was king, people had to have food to eat. Eventually, technology such as the heavy plow would improve agricultural yields and quality of life. The evolution of the plow from a pointed stick pulled by a draft animal that broke the soil so that a farmer could plant may have worked for light soil, but Europe had its share of harder soils that resistant plowing. The heavy plow, with wheels that supported a sturdier blade, was first used in Asia; approximately 400 years later, by 600 CE, Europe had the new equipment, which led to an increase in harvests and population.

The water mill, another technological innovation which was familiar to the Greeks and Romans but took longer to become part of the Early Middle Ages farming tradition, was firmly in place by the turn of the ninth century. The apparatus, which used a turning wheel whose water-catching paddles provided a reliable source of power that could operate machinery, was in place all over the world. Adaptations meant that the new source of power could be used to power paper mills, blast furnaces, forge mills, and tanneries. Technology was refining the industry of the era and by the inception of the High Middle Ages around 1000 CE, that transformation would be established.

Political disarray was beginning to find order as skilled military leaders plied their ruthless craft against their enemies. This was seen in England in the late 9th century, where Alfred the Great of Wessex was able to enforce a treaty which contained the Vikings into a region known as the Danelaw. It was true on the Continent as well. The alchemy of conquest and geography led to the gold of nationhood, dramatically shown by the Carolingians, who used their power as mayors to eventually rise to the kingship of the Frankish lands.

Beginning in the middle of the fifth century, a dynasty arose to rule over what had been ancient Gaul and other Roman provinces in Francia, now France, including the southern part of Germania. Under the Merovingian Clovis I, all of Gaul was united. Before that, his father, Childeric I had defeated the armies of the Visigoths and Saxons.

Clovis converted to his wife's Christian faith. His kingdom was divided among his four sons, a pattern which continued over the following century. The family members may have battled among themselves, but they were a powerful force against outsiders. As time went on, the role of the king diminished, not only because power was divided among sons, but also because political power was delegated to the mayors of the palace. One of these mayors, known as either Pepin the Short or Pepin the Younger due to a mistranslation, became the political ruler—not king—of the Franks; his sons inherited the position; a single king ruled, but the power in the realm belonged to the sons of the mayor, who were frequently ambitious. Pepin ruled for a long time. His son Charles Martel had tested his battle skills against other nobles and even his stepmother, but the military efforts took on a broader significance in 732 when he went to battle at Tours, defeating the Muslims and bringing their expansion into Europe to a halt. Under Charles the Hammer, as he was known after his victory against a powerful and previously undefeated foe, European structure began to take shape in the Middle Ages as knighthood and feudalism became two of the dominant social movements of the era.

The figurehead kings were no match for the ruthless descendants of Pepin and in 751, Pope Zachary sanctioned the rise to kingship of Charles Martel's son Pepin III, displacing the last Merovingian king Childeric in order to provide the land of the Franks a strong ruler to curb the rebellion on its borders. Accepting the title of king made Charles Martel's son ruler over what is now continental Western Europe north of the Pyrenees Mountains.

At this time, Europe was a collection of small kingdoms ruled by military leaders who rose to power through their feats and their command over their followers. The Carolingians knew how to fight, but they needed to be able to support cavalry forces. By being able to allocate land to loyal followers, the king could count on having a military force that could respond to dangers. In return, the vassals paid homage to their liege lord and received land, or a fief. The bond between lord and vassal came out of the land: the nation and its king were protected by the soldiers who would take to arms when danger arose that threatened. The beginnings of nationhood were taking form.

Charles the Great

In 800, a leader arose who would recreate not merely a nation, but a semblance of empire. His name was Charles, but history knows him as Charles the Great, or Charlemagne. He was given the title of Holy Roman Emperor by Pope Leo III, a nod to the long-last empire that had fallen in 476. Charlemagne's rule begin in 768 when his father died; the kingdom went to Charlemagne and his brother, but the death of Carloman left Charles as the sole ruler. He was a man of his times; in defense of his Christianity, he forced the Saxons that he defeated in battle to convert.

Charlemagne's partnership with the Church and his promotion of the arts, religion and culture had the blessing of the Pope. The Carolingian ruler was able to do something the Romans hadn't: vanquish the Germanic resistance, extending his realm nearly to the Russian steppes.

Charlemagne had a vision that was based on more than conquest. It's to the new emperor's credit that he made education a priority. Charles himself was barely able to read and write, and he regarded these skills as so important that he kept writing tablets close by so that he could practice his letters. He depended upon his literate courtiers and officials to read to him. He wanted more for his children, of which there were many: there might have been as 18 sons and daughters from a number of wives and mistresses. He was already acquainted with men of learning, most notably Alcuin of York, who had accompanied the headmaster of the cathedral school in

York on his travels. Alcuin's erudition was highly regarded; he was a teacher, but he also wrote Bible commentaries and biographies of the saints. Charlemagne's ambition was for a palace school for his children and the offspring of his nobles, and he needed a teacher who could bring the highest level of learning.

Alcuin was reluctant at first, but he agreed to take on the task. He established a library and created lesson plans, spearheading educational reforms that would endure and expand. Charlemagne decreed that the monks would take on the role of educators, teaching young boys to read and write. They would be educated so that they, in time, could serve the monastery. Uniform Christine theology would be taught. Eventually, Charlemagne expanded the range by having the monasteries take on the education of the boys in the district, not just to provide future monks for holy orders, but to develop learning in ordinary people. Some subject matter was religious in nature, but the monks also taught Plato, legal writing, and Germanic legends. Making education available to those who were not intended for the priesthood or born to the nobility was a revolutionary direction.

The need for teachers was crucial; the supply was limited. In comparison, Ireland had a well-developed monastic tradition. Irish missionaries spread the Christian faith to Scotland, England, and Europe. Perhaps the most outstanding achievement of the Irish monasteries was their talent in illustrating manuscripts, particularly the Book of Kells. Irish monks were at the forefront of the educational reforms that were based in monasteries and their presence kept the light of learning bright in the regions where they traveled.

Charlemagne's passion for order compelled him to follow the Irish example, leading to the adoption of uniform curriculum and students learned a standardized form of Latin. A type of calligraphy established a uniform writing style, producing religious texts for public worship as well as private devotions, along with the classical texts that were showing up all over Europe.

What is remarkable is that these reforms were not restricted to the clergy, or the nobles, but to the common people. It would be an exaggeration to say that this was the foundation of Western democracy but an acknowledgment of its roots must be made and Charlemagne deserves credit for prioritizing education as a vital building block in a stable society.

Charlemagne's Legacy

But Charlemagne's empire didn't last; he died in 814. By 843, the empire was divided by the Treaty of Verdun into three segments to provide realms for the three surviving sons of Charlemagne's heir, Louis the Pious. The man who is regarded by some historians as the Father of Europe, who ruled over what is present-day Belgium, Luxembourg, France, western Germany and the Netherlands, who established a solid bond between political power and the role of the church so that the Christian faith was intertwined with power in Europe, had made his mark but his dynasty was short-lived. His legacy, however, had a much longer life span.

The support of education was of great benefit to society. Another innovation which the Carolingians originated was feudalism. Manors in the Middle Ages were small communities; on the estate was the castle where the lord and family lived. The village and the church were part of manor life, and they were more or less self-contained, although there were sometimes visitors such as traveling peddlers, pilgrims, and bards. The villeins, or serfs, depended upon the lord of the manor to protect them in exchange for their work upon the land. In turn, the lords of the manor, as vassals of the king, owed the throne military support which they provided with soldiers.

By the end of the Early Middle Ages, the indeterminate boundaries of the regions abandoned by Rome had taken the form of national borders. Alliances were formed, political marriages were made, and enemies and rivalries began to dictate policy. Over it all was the Christian Church, providing spiritual leadership that also lent itself to martial pursuits when the ecclesiastical authorities deemed that God's will sought blood. Power was its brand, absolute authority its trademark. Yet not all Christians in the High Middle Ages would interpret the word of God in the same way that the papal authorities did.

Chapter Three
The High Middle Ages

The 11th century was a turning point of the Middle Ages. Rome was the distant past. The political organization that replaced the barbarian invasions of earlier centuries helped to nurture a political stability which European had not known since the Romans were in control. While the Romans had been gone for centuries, their political heirs, particularly the Franks and the English, were independent nations who consolidated their own boundaries. Populations began to increase around the 12th century and with more people came economic prosperity. Charlemagne's educational reforms were marvelous innovations, but the 12th century would go further with the development of universities in Bologna, Oxford, Paris and Modena. In some parts of Western Europe, the early sparks of the Renaissance would already begin to blaze by the 12th century in some countries.

Christianity no longer competed in Europe with the gods of the Northmen, or the Britons, or the Welsh; instead, Christians competed among themselves for the souls of the believers. By the time of the High Middle Ages, roughly from the year 1000 to 1300, the average citizen could not have imagined a world in which the Church was not a dominant factor. Secular life was thoroughly permeated by the sacred: arts and architecture reflected the inspiration of faith; education, although it expanded into secular directions, was nonetheless based upon traditional beliefs. Even war would act upon the direction of the Church leaders to maintain the purity of the faith. Yet no matter how holy their intentions, men were men; when a kingdom was at stake, even a practicing Christian could put the Sermon on the Mount aside to rely on his sword and his soldiers.

In England, the kingdom of the Anglo-Saxons, which had defeated and contained their Viking invaders, faced a new, powerful foe across the English Channel. Robert, Duke of Normandy, was a bachelor, but he was not without an heir. His illegitimate son William was a powerful and capable leader. The Anglo-Saxons and Normans had family ties in common, but when the English king Edward the Confessor died in 1066, the ruling House of Wessex came to an end. In Normandy, Edward's cousin William had his eyes on the English throne. Edward may have promised him the kingship, but Edward might also have promised it to the powerful Harold Godwinson, an Anglo-Saxon. When William landed in England, Harold, who had already fought a battle against Norwegian invaders in September, had to plunge back into battle in October. The Anglo-Saxons were defeated, and the Normans were masters of England.

The Bayeux Tapestry

The Early Middle Ages are not readily recognized for their contributions to the world of art, although that would change as the centuries moved the people further away from hardscrabble survival. However, one memorable work is also a historical record. The Bayeux Tapestry tells the story of the Norman Conquest in cloth panels with 70 scenes depicting the historical events which led to the Battle of Hastings. The tapestry commemorating a battle that took place in 1066 is dated to 1092, but the workmanship, as well as the theme, of this tapestry has preserved its timelessness.

The legend connects the tapestry with Matilda, wife of William the Conqueror, but there's no basis in fact for this belief. Yet other people from William's life are referred to in the tapestry, including Odo the Bishop of Bayeux, William's half-brother, as 70 meters of cloth spin the story of the battle that changed England's destiny.

William's name is also associated with a famous book, although none could call it a work of art. Completed in 1086, two decades after the battle that gave William the English throne, the Domesday Book is a record of a survey of both England and Wales in order to investigate which taxes were due to William's predecessor. By recording how much each landowner owned in land and livestock, and what those assets were worth in turn, William intended to find out just how much his new holdings were worth. There was no escaping the royal acquisitive eye. As Richard FitzNeal, an administrative official in the court of Henry King II explained in 1179, "for as the sentence of that strict and terrible last account cannot be evaded by any skillful subterfuge, so when this book is appealed to ... its sentence cannot be quashed or set aside with impunity. That is why we have called the book 'the Book of Judgement' ... because its decisions, like those of the Last Judgment, are unalterable."

Agriculture

It's easy to look upon an era and define it in terms of its leaders and inventions. The High Middle Ages had its share of both. However, another development which was to have a profound effect on the time period does not always receive its share of credit. A period of warmer climate that began in the tenth century would last for nearly four centuries until the Little Ice Age brought colder temperatures to Europe. Thanks to these initial warmer temperatures, wheat could be grown north as far as Scandinavia and grapes for wine were cultivated in northern England. Greater crop yields and more food were as strengthening to the population as standing armies, leading to an increase in industry that built up the economies of the region as towns developed and trade prospered.

A relatively stable political environment was matched with innovations in agriculture that led to a more secure food supply. This would eventually transform the social structure of feudalism which dominated the early Middle Ages from the time of the Carolingians. Lands which had been wilderness after Rome fell were cleared and became home to the people who settled there. Food production also increased during this time as new ways of farming were introduced, including the use of a heavier plow, horses instead of oxen, and a three-field crop rotation system that cultivated a wider variety of crops than the previous two-field system. Planting legumes nurtured the soil by preventing nitrogen from being depleted. The cultivation of beans meant that a balanced diet for all social classes enhanced health for the first time in history.

This increased population contributed to the founding of new towns and an increase in industrial and economic activity during the period. Economic power began to shift from the eastern Mediterranean to Western Europe. A merchant class began to develop. Towns grew and flourished, travel and communication became faster and safer. As the population increased, feudalism would decline.

Some ties to the land would nurture crops which would prove to have lasting appeal for all ages. Distillation, which had been developed by Greece and Egypt, led to the production of liquors such as Irish whisky and German brandy during the High Middle Ages, as the people learned how to sufficiently heat the liquid and separate its individual components as they boiled at different temperatures.

The Crusades

It was not only alcohol that separated when heated. Differences in doctrinal interpretation and culture had been heating up between Christianity's theological offspring. The Eastern and Western factions of the Christian Church split in 1054 into Western Catholicism and Eastern Orthodoxy. Their leaders, Pope Leo IX and Patriarch Michael I, excommunicated each other in a dispute over papal authority. The stability of the Christian Church which had held Western Europe together during the difficult Early Middle Ages would show fissures in its former unity.

The Romans had legions. The Middle Ages had religion. Put them together and the Crusades, the quest to reclaim the holy city of Jerusalem that was the foundation of Christianity, were inevitable. In 1095, the Pope called upon Christians to go to war, building a groundswell of religious zeal. For several centuries, popes would continue to call upon their flocks to fight the infidel.

Islamic society had advanced tremendously from its sixth century origins and in many ways had become more advanced than that of the Europeans. By the 8th century, the Chinese invention of paper was being used in the Islamic world to produce books. Soap, windmills, surgical instruments, and Arabic numerals were in use. Cultural diversity displayed itself as texts from Greek, Iranian and Indian works were translated into Arabic. Cairo, Baghdad, and Damascus were great cities where scholarship advanced.

With the rise of Islam, Christianity was not the only monotheistic faith to command loyalty of believers. Yet for Christians, the Muslims were the enemy; heretics who controlled the Holy Land where Jesus and his disciples had lived, preached, and died.

Western Europe was now a political entity by the end of the 11th century, less polished and powerful than the Byzantine Empire in the East or the Islamic Empire of the Middle East and North Africa. However, the Byzantine Empire was showing its age, coming out on the losing end in battles that cost it territory.

In 1095, The Emperor Alexius Comnenus asked Pope Urban II for assistance against the Turks. East and West cast suspicious eyes against one another, but they were

Christians united against a Muslim enemy. The Pope asked for soldiers to come to the aid of the Byzantines to recapture the Holy Land, and the response was wildly enthusiastic. Knights had been part of the social structure since the 10th century, a position which would increase in prominence and legend throughout the Middle Ages, but even ordinary men felt the lure of holy war. Crusades to win back the Holy Land would become an ongoing mission, although ultimately an unsuccessful one, of the papacy into the 15th century.

The power plays among the leaders of the Crusade began almost instantly. When the Western armies landed in Constantinople, Emperor Alexius required the leaders to swear loyalty to him and recognize his authority over lands they would regain from the Turks, or any other lands that would fall under their command. Relations between the Eastern and Western leaders would not improve, but the army went forth, attacking the cities of Nicea and Antioch. Then it was on to Jerusalem, which was occupied by the Fatimids of Egypt, followers of the Shi'ite tradition, who were the enemies of the Seljuks, who were Sunni. The Christians besieged Jerusalem in 1099; when the city surrendered, the Christians, in the name of Christ, slaughtered the civilians inside.

Feeling that they had achieved their goal, many of the Crusaders returned home. As pilgrims in later years traveled to Jerusalem as part of their religious observations, they often were threatened by bandits and robbers. An order of knights that came to be known as the Knights Templar formed to protect the travelers. This order would become very wealthy; ultimately perceived as a threat to the established authorities, the Templars would be forced to disband in the early 14th century.

Yet Crusades to the Holy Land would continue to be both hobby and rite of passage for subsequent generations of Christians. Some of the ones who would answer the call included Richard the Lionheart, King Louis VII of France and his dazzling bride Eleanor of Aquitaine, King Conrad III of Germany, Philip II and Louis IX of France.

Chapter Four
The Flowering of the Church

As spiritual faith grew, it found expression in physical structures. Gothic architecture, which began to gain popularity in the 1200 CE, expressed the effect that religion had on the arts. Cathedrals which took centuries to build had flying buttresses, spires, arches, pointed vaults, and stained glass windows. The term "Gothic" was a term of contempt because it was not classical Roman nor Greek, and the prejudice against the barbarians who had ruined Rome extended to the architecture which they created. However, the churches, cathedrals, and castles that were constructed in this style gave the Middle Ages a medieval logo that expressed the power of Christian faith.

The church had a strong influence on literature, but not all works had a religious inspiration. Writing in the 11th century, Geoffrey of Monmouth's stories about King Arthur would carry the legends of Camelot to the highest social circles and royal courts. Written in 1133, Geoffrey's Historia Regum Britanniae told the tale of Arthur, whose court at Camelot included the finest, most gallant knights of the realm. Other writers including Cretien de Troyes and Marie de France added to the tales which established the tradition of courtly love.

Because marriages were arranged for political and economic reasons and alliances, the inspiration for courtly love did not depend upon matrimony to be authentic and passionate, as the courtly lover and his lady were not expected to consummate their love. The chivalric lover would strive to be worthy of his lady love, going on quests and living through ordeals to prove his devotion to her. One of the most famous women of the era, Eleanor of Aquitaine, was a patroness of the movement, and while she may not have experienced much courtly love, she certainly knew a great deal about the affairs of the heart.

Eleanor of Aquitaine

One of the most celebrated women of the Middle Ages, Eleanor inherited the rich and prosperous duchy of Aquitaine at the age of 15 upon the death of her father. Her inheritance made her a matrimonial prize; before long, she was betrothed to the heir of the French throne, Louis, who became the king within weeks after the wedding. When her husband answered the Pope's call to crusade, Eleanor joined him. Although the couple had two daughters, the marriage was a failure, and they were granted an annulment in 1152. However, Eleanor would not remain unmarried for long.

Two months after annulling her royal husband, Eleanor wed Henry, Count of Anjou, Duke of Normandy, and future king of England. This union was productive, providing eight children to serve as heirs and matrimonial prospects. Henry was a capable leader whose territory has been called the Angevin Empire, including not only

England but much of Wales and part of Ireland, and also the western portion of France. Not only had Henry taken Louis's wife, but he also had French lands. Henry was not a faithful husband, but fidelity was not expected to be a royal attribute. Whatever his marital flaws, Henry's tireless energy was poured into stabilizing the country that had been left in chaos after years of civil war as King Stephen and the Empress Matilda, Henry's mother, fought for the throne.

Henry liked power, he liked order, and he liked supremacy. His chancellor, Thomas Becket, had proven successful in the job; when the archbishopric of Canterbury fell vacant, Henry II saw his friend as the perfect candidate for the position. Confident of Becket's loyalty, Henry assumed that his archbishop would provide him with the influence over the Church that he sought.

However, when Becket donned his clerical robes, he pledged his loyalty to the Pope rather than King Henry. The Church was allowed to try clerics in religious, rather than civil courts, and Henry opposed this tradition – a point of view that Becket did not hold. In 1163, when an ecclesiastical court acquitted a cleric who was accused of murder, Becket supported the church's decision. Wary of the king's wrath, he then fled to France. The discord was eventually smoothed over and seven years later, Becket returned to Canterbury and to controversy as he denied absolution to two bishops he had excommunicated for supporting the king in the previous decision. Infuriated, the king went into a rage—and Henry's royal rages were akin to fits—and he was said to have demanded why none of the men of his court would rid him of that meddlesome priest.

Four knights accepted the challenge, went to the cathedral in Canterbury and killed Becket with their swords. Henry was forced to do penance for his role in the murder, and Becket was canonized.

Henry was tempestuous in all his interactions. So was Eleanor. Their incendiary romance set the marriage ablaze into ashes and Eleanor set up her own household in Poitiers in 1167, where her encouragement of the tenets of courtly love nurtured a chivalric tradition that influenced music, literature, and the arts as well as social habits. Ballads were sung, poems were memorized and recited, and knights and ladies played out the roles of the tradition; a knight wore his lady's favors in jousting tournaments, those mock battles where knights practiced their skills.

Before long, Eleanor's adherence to the symbolic pastime of courtly love would be replaced by her loyalty to her sons. The heir, Young Henry, plotted against his father and aimed to seize Henry II's throne. Deciding that his wife was part of the conspiracy, Henry II imprisoned her in England, but incarceration did not isolate her from conspiracies in support of her sons against their father. After Henry's death, Eleanor served as regent while the heir, Richard I, fulfilled his promise to go on the Third Crusade. Eleanor remained active in Richard's reign as well as that of his heir, her youngest son John. Late in her long life, she entered the abbey at Fontevraud and died in 1204, which was a pity, as John could have used her advice during his troubled reign.

Heresy

During the Early Middle Ages, the ninth century saw the effect that two Christian monarchs, Alfred the Great of Wessex and the Holy Roman Emperor Charlemagne, had on promoting education in their countries as they supported the efforts of the monasteries to develop centers of learning. The High Middle Ages saw those efforts bear fruit.

The works of Aristotle were rediscovered by European scholars in the 11th century; Islam's libraries provided resources for Europeans to acquaint themselves with ancient philosophers and then to continue the intellectual efforts. Thomas Aquinas developed a school of thought which held that the mind at birth was a blank slate with the ability to think that came from the divine spark. Other medieval scholars whose works broadened philosophy included Peter Abelard, Francisco Suarez, Duns Scotus, Roscellinus of Compiegne, Anselm of Canterbury, William of Ockham, and Bernard of Clairvaux. Philosophy in these times was never devoid of a religious context and as the scholars became more learned, the teachings of the church were contested by men of astonishing brilliance.

Peter Abelard was a charismatic teacher in Paris whose intellect drew crowds of students. When he was in his thirties, he entered into a romantic love affair with another scholar, Héloïse d'Argenteuil, the niece of canon Fulbert. Fulbert tried to keep the lovers apart but they defied him and found ways to meet furtively. When Héloïse became pregnant, she went to live in Brittany with Abelard's family. Her son was named Astrolabe, after the scientific instrument invented by Muslims. The couple married secretly, but Fulbert made the marriage public and Abelard sent his wife to the convent where she had grown up in order to protect her from her uncle.

Héloïse did not have a vocation for the cloister. Her uncle, convinced that Abelard was trying to get out of his matrimonial obligations, had him castrated. After this grisly turn of events, Abelard decided to become a monk. His intellect was as powerful as ever, but his teachings and his arrogance repeatedly brought him into conflict with church teachings. In 1140, when his teachings were believed to contain heresies, he was brought to the attention of Bernard of Clairvaux, an abbot and reformer who founded an order of Cistercians in 1115 which proved to be immensely popular and influential.

Pope Innocent II sided with Bernard of Clairvaux and Abelard was threatened with excommunication and a sentence of perpetual silence, his books to be burned and he himself confined to a monastery. When an ally, Peter the Venerable intervened, Abelard was permitted to go to the priory of St Marcle, where he died in 1142.

This would not be the last time that Bernard of Clairvaux would be called upon to combat heretical ideas in the church; his reputation as a reformer and his standing of high ecclesiastical esteem would remain a resource as the issue of heresy continued to batter at the orthodoxy of the Catholic Church.

The Cathars

As scholarship matured, it often came into conflict with the church's orthodoxy, which had a limited capacity to tolerate challenges. The rise of the mendicant orders was not heresy, but was a reaction to the ostentatious and elaborate image of the church. In the 12th century, the Franciscans, Dominicans, Carmelites, and Augustinians espoused a simple form of the faith which was based on poverty, obedience, and service. They were movements which did not seek to challenge church doctrine. The heresies of others exemplified the ways in which the church-centered rural society was being changed by the influence and changing perspectives of the growing urban culture.

The Cathars were members of a Christian movement based in southern Europe that was denounced by the Roman Catholic Church for their view that God was both good and evil. The Church authorities sent missionaries to combat the views which were in opposition to the accepted doctrine which saw God as solely good, but when the missionaries failed to convert the Cathars, the Pope went to war against them. When the French king could not lead the force, he authorized one of his barons, Simon de Montfort, to undertake the Albigensian Crusade. Thousands of Cathars were slaughtered; later, when the Pope initiated the Inquisition in 1234 to address the crisis, more Cathars were burned at the stake.

The Roman Catholic Church was determined to speak with one voice. As the Middle Ages matured, there were often many voices raised in opposition to papal authority.

That chorus of dissent would grow louder with time, drowning out the imposing call of the Church.

Chapter Five

Times of Change

THE MAGNA CARTA

No one disputes that King John, the last of the sons of Henry II and Eleanor of Aquitaine, was a bad king. John was dishonest, cowardly, sadistic, sexually aggressive, excommunicated from the church, and greedy. His unsuccessful war against France led to the loss of Normandy and Anjou. He was so bad a king that the barons of his own nation decided that they could not endure his tyranny. In 1215, the English barons presented the king with a document known as the Magna Carta, or Great Charter, which set the bold step of requiring monarchs to obey the laws of the land. The Magna Carta also promised to protect the rights of the church, as well as limit the amount that was owed to the church in feudal payments. It would provide the barons with swift justice and protection from illegal imprisonment. The document was annulled by Pope Innocent III, inciting the First Barons' War, but the Magna Carta, although it was aimed to protect the rights of the powerful landed gentry, was a cornerstone in a movement toward human rights and is regarded as the first written constitution in Europe.

Trade, Towns and Travel

Perceptions about the privileged were a long way from incorporating equality, but the evolution toward a merchant class was altering the social structure of the citizens. With the growth of towns came the creation of guilds, organizations which were a combination of trade union and community center. The members of these guilds not only honed their skills as craftsmen but they also expanded into entertainment, providing theatre performances based on Bible stories, particularly stories which had a connection to their profession.

As towns flourished and merchants expanded their roles in the economy, trade not only maximized the geography of an area but also exposed its residents to products and tastes beyond the physical boundaries of their nations. In the mid-twelfth century, the Hanseatic League, which was formed by cities including Amsterdam, Berlin, Bruges, Gdansk, Konigsberg, Bergen, Novgorod, Bremen, Hanover, and Cologne, formed with the ambition of promoting trade by means of the waterways. The Crusades turned into more than just a battle between opposing religions convinced that each alone was the true faith. Trade routes that opened as a result of the Crusades brought Europeans a taste for novelties such as olive oil, spices and new textiles, while ports became more important to the economy of the nation.

With trade came travel, and Marco Polo of Venice wrote of his adventures along China's Silk Road, enthralling readers who could not imagine such opulence or such hardship. Born in Venice in 1254, Marco Polo belonged to a family of jewel merchants whose clientele was in Asia. Their stay in the court of Kublai Khan exposed the Venetians to a level of wealth and sophistication that made it obvious that Europe's roots were still comparatively provincial. Traveling with his uncle and father in 1271, Marco Polo was fascinated by the sights of the exotic Middle East and Asia. Some of the remarkable innovations which Polo witnessed during his travels included the use of paper money for gold and silver; coal as a source of heating fuel; and an efficient system of correspondence that included first class and second class mail delivery. His account of his travels not only influenced cartographers but also inspired Christopher Columbus, who would also set sail to explore an unknown world.

Innovations

Europe was eager and willing to incorporate the technology of the ancient world into its working routine. The spinning wheel was brought from India in the 13th century and became a mainstay of the household. The compass, which came into use late in the 12th century, would prove useful as the Europeans began to explore the oceans. Arabic numerals were adopted in Europe in 1202. Italy was at the cutting edge of innovation, inventing eyeglasses sometime in the 1280s; the decade before saw Italy manufacturing paper. Even earlier, windmills were in use in England in 1185.

Once again, the church earns praise for its role in the development of music notation, which began in religious institutions. Guido of Arezzo was one of the early creators of the notation, which helped singers remember the notes for Gregorian chants.

Europe was poised for an outburst of creativity which would transform the arts. The Late Middle Ages would establish the foundation for this metamorphosis, but those years would also witness much turmoil, disease, and suffering.

Chapter Six
The Late Middle Ages

What was the Late Middle Ages in some parts of Europe was actually the Renaissance for others, where the learning and the arts had, like a precocious child, advanced to new heights while slower nation-siblings took a longer time to master the knack. The Late Middle Ages led to the invention of the printing press, the publication of Dante's Divine Comedy, the expansion of trade and the growth of cities which would become powerful in their own right. But the era was also shadowed by the bubonic plague, the start of the 100 Years' War, and the unbelievable career of Joan of Arc. Feudalism would wane, and so would that stronghold of spiritual power, the Roman Catholic Church.

In contrast, the High Middle Ages had been good for Europe. Advances in agriculture had fed a continent; people who moved from farms to towns invigorated the economy, improved standards of living, and played midwife to dynamic cultural and artistic prowess. The Church had been involved in controversies, but its power was absolute, and as long as a believer remained orthodox in practices, there was nothing to fear. But new ways of thinking by people who were willing to die for their beliefs would forever alter the balance of religious power in the Christian world.

Famine

Thanks to progressive agricultural technology and practices, the High Middle Ages had enjoyed greater food production, a great boon for an expanding population. There were 100 million people living in Europe by the year 1300; 15 cities in Europe had populations greater than 50,000. Some of this progress was a result of the warming trend that had affected Europe during the period from 950-1250. But soon those benign temperatures would change and what historians call The Little Ice Age, lasting from 1300-1350, would bring colder temperatures to the Continent. Then, in 1315, famine struck Europe's northern countries. For two years, crop failures brought starvation, leading to the deaths of more than a million people. For two years, the population of Europe suffered from disease and starvation; the lack of food engendered insecurity which in turn gave rise to social unrest, as both peasants and nobles alike found their worlds changing.

The Black Death

Time moved slowly in an era where the sun remained the most common means of telling time. Yet events were moving faster and they would affect the health and well-being of Europe. Travel was not as slow and laborious as it had been in earlier times, and the ease of trade meant that communities were no longer isolated from the outside world. The conquests by Mongols had facilitated travel between East and West. However, one of the most significant exports from Asia would also be the most deadly. Rats were a factor of everyday life in the Middle Ages; likewise, fleas. No one then realized that the fleas which lived on the rats were themselves feeding bacteria; no one would have known that the terrible and dreaded disease that would kill from 25 percent to 45 percent of Europe's population between 1347 and 1350 was the fault of an unseen pestilence. Nor would the disease vanish once the pandemic ended; instead, it would periodically revisit Europe, bringing death and apprehension in its wake.

Victims didn't last long, but their deaths were agonizing. Respiratory failure led to the victims' skin turning purplish-black. The cities which had blossomed through trade's expansion were the front lines of the plague's progress, facilitating the spread of the dreaded disease.

Progress in science and learning did not nullify the fears and superstitions of a population which saw divine cause in disaster. Was the world coming to an end? Was God angry at his people for their sins? Was this catastrophe the fault of the Jews, who were perennially blamed for the world's ills?

The Black Death, or bubonic plague, was first seen in Asia but in 1346 it reached the shore of the Black Sea; soon, merchants from Italy carried the disease home. The disease broke out in October 1347 in Messina and infected the entire peninsula by April of the following year. When it arrived in Paris in 1348, there were 800 people a day dying from the disease. The front lines of the plague's progress were the cities, those growing, thriving, crowded centers of population. To put the number of deaths in perspective, by 1351, the population had been devastated; it was the equivalent of what the numbers would be if everyone in California, Texas, Illinois, New York, Pennsylvania, and Florida had died. It would take 150 years for the population to return to its former numbers. The loss of life led to the loss of labor and scarcity of food. The ones who were most affected by this, the peasantry, were desperate.

The Peasants' Revolt

Foreshadowing a revolution against the French nobility which would take place four hundred years in the future, French peasants known as the Jacquerie attacked the affluent leaders of society until they were in turn executed by the wealthy nobles and their monarch. In Kent, England, Wat Tyler and followers carried out a rebellion in 1381 against the poll tax and destroyed the property records to emphasize their economic straits. The rebels met with the young King Richard II, who promised to provide free trade, the abolition of serfdom and forced labor, and cheap land, but as a fourteen-year old, he could not force his government to follow through on the promises he had given, and the peasants continued their rampage. At a second meeting with the king, Tyler was killed. Ultimately the rebellion was put down after a month. Yet the lone victory remained: the poll tax was not levied.

The Hundred Years' War

The Hundred Years' War began in 1337, when the English monarchs went to war against France to establish their rights to the French throne. Intermarriage and conquest had blurred the lines of ownership over the centuries, and it would take more than a century for the property lines to be resolved. When the war ended in 1453, a dynasty of 300 years was brought down, replaced by monarchs who would change the very core of the nation of England.

For centuries, England and France had shared bloodlines, intermarried into dynasties, sworn allegiance and conquered each other's territories. The 14th century saw an extended period of war that actually lasted longer than 100 years as England and France battled. The irony of this conflict is that the duration of the battles themselves actually lasted less than one month.

Edward the Black Prince was the son of the ill-fated Edward II and the grandson of Edward I, an effective and victorious military leader. His victory over the French yielded territory and power at Poitiers in 1356. Fifty years later, Henry V defeated a French force at the famed battle of Agincourt and married into the French royal family.

The English and their archers were buoyed by a sense of triumph; the French were humiliated. But where their armor and their armies had failed, a peasant girl could succeed - a peasant girl named Jeanne. Known to history as Joan of Arc, she claimed to have heard the voice of God when she was 12 years old. Four years later, the divine voice directed her to aid the Dauphin, Charles VII, who served as regent because of the insanity of his father the king. Charles provided a small military force for the girl, who, wearing armor and short hair, was able to break the siege at Orleans, forcing the English to leave in 1429. In 1430, treachery by the Burgundians, who had taken sides with the English, delivered the Maid of Orleans to the

English military. Regarded as a heretic, she was tried by French priests who supported the English side, found guilty of witchcraft, and burned at the stake for her crimes.

Eventually, the French were able to retain their lands and the English returned home in 1453. For England, though, the epoch of war would continue, though not against the French. Instead the Houses of York and Lancaster, each claiming the English throne, battled against each other. In 1485, the last Plantagenet king of England, a dynasty that had begun when Henry II took the throne, was supplanted by the Tudors.

Along with the Tudors, new names would appear in the Late Middle Ages. In Florence, Italy, a wealthy banking family known as the Medici rose to prominence. Lorenzo the Magnificent was a supporter of the arts whose patronage of Leonardo da Vinci, Michelangelo, and Botticelli would signal the arrival of the Renaissance.

Chapter Seven

The End and the Beginning

Literature, both religious and secular, flourished in the Late Middle Ages. Julian of Norwich, an English mystic, wrote Revelations of Divine Love in 1395. This was the first book known to have been written by female author. She was not the only female whose written works gave women a voice in a period of time when they were often both illiterate and silent: Clare of Assisi, Bridget of Sweden, and Catherine of Siena, all nuns, also wrote of their beliefs.

In the hands of a master, even literature with a religious foundation could appeal to a broad audience of people seeking entertainment as well as enlightenment. Dante Alighieri finished his epic poem, the Divine Comedy, in 1320; the story of his journey through Hell, Purgatory, and Heaven is an allegory of the Christian soul's search for God. His guide to Heaven is Beatrice, a woman from Florence adored by Dante in the popular courtly tradition.

Less ethereal and more robust than works of a religious theme, Geoffrey's Chaucer's Canterbury Tales, the rollicking story of a group of pilgrims, consists of 24 stories by the pilgrims who entertain one another as they travel. Chaucer wrote his characters as real people with personalities that are earthy and engaging, displaying human nature in its nobility and its vice. Chaucer's profession was not a writer; he was the controller of customs, justice of the peace and then clerk of the English king's court. He had a unique view into the lives of the English nobility and royalty because his wife was the sister of Katherine Swynford, the lover and later third wife of John of Gaunt, one of Edward III's sons. The Swynford union would produce the Beauforts, which in turn would sire the Tudor dynasty.

Religion

Christianity and Islam continued as foes through the Late Middle Ages. In 1389, the Ottoman Turks conquered Serbia and Bulgaria; in 1448, the Turks defeated a Hungarian army and absorbed the fallen Byzantine Empire. The mighty Roman Empire, which had survived in the East, was no more and was no longer Christian. With the trade routes to the East cut off, Europe needed to find new routes. Need inspired exploration, as Christopher Columbus and Vasco de Gama would eventually set sail for new shores.

The series of Crusades which began in 1095, when the Pope responded to the request of the Christian emperor of the Byzantines to rid the Holy Land of the Muslim control, came to an end in 1487. Crusaders who had gone to fight in the name of Jesus Christ because the Pope promised that soldiers in this holy war would be absolved of their sins achieved some victories: the opening of the Mediterranean benefitted trade, allowing the Italian city-states of Venice and Genoa to prosper. To Catholics, the Crusades were a manifestation of the Church's quest to serve God. Yet the Protestant movement, which had been growing in number as the Late Middle Ages came to a close, saw the Crusades as additional proof that the papacy had subverted the holy gospels into a malignant expression of political power.

Late in the 14th century, the Lollard movement became popular. Based on the lectures of John Wycliffe, a priest whose views directly challenged the foundation of Catholic dogma, the movement revolved around the concept that personal interpretation of the Bible was a fundamental guide for living in accordance with God's laws. Wycliffe disagreed with the Church's stance on good works; he opposed the elevated status of the clergy and their luxurious lifestyles. He also believed that the Bible should be translated into the languages that ordinary people spoke. After his death, Wycliffe's body was exhumed and burned, his writings were banned and likewise burned, and he was declared a heretic. Yet he would not be the last dissenter who would confront the established church on its views. On the horizon was a German Catholic priest whose writings would be so influential that the Catholic Church's monopoly on Christian faith in Europe would come to an end. The Protestant standard, initially borne by Martin Luther, would win adherents.

Innovations

Despite the privations, conflicts, and devastation of the Late Middle Ages, European civilization made great strides toward the Renaissance, one of the most monumental periods of time in human history. The hourglass was a utilitarian piece of technology which made it possible to measure the passage of time. Mechanical clocks would eventually replace the hourglass, but until then, the hourglass served a useful purpose for everyone from cooks timing a meal to clerics leading a worship service.

It could be argued that the most influential innovation to emerge from the Late Middle Ages was the printing press, invented by Johannes Gutenberg in 1440. Mass production of printed material meant that more books, pamphlets, and articles could be disseminated to more people. The accessibility of printed material helped literacy and learning to expand. With the cost of producing books so dramatically reduced, people who had ideas to spread would be able to do so quickly and affordably. The use of paper, rather than calfskin or sheepskin, was a timesaver and a cost saver. With printing no longer regimented by the control of the Catholic Church, ideas contrary to orthodox doctrine could no longer be suppressed.

Conclusion

The Middle Ages was clearly much more than a time of filler. The voice of the ordinary person was heard in ways never before experienced. For all its awkward, cumbersome, uncertain steps toward the development of self-government and individuality, the era provided civilization with an unforgettable roster of actors whose roles continue to reverberate in our modern times, just as they would preface the bold speech of the Renaissance to follow.

About the Author

At Hourly History, we focus on publishing history books that are concise, straightforward and take no longer than one hour to read.

Receive our new eBooks for free every Friday.
Sign up at: www.hourlyhistory.com/free

Made in the USA
Middletown, DE
04 June 2021